Get set... GO!

Collage

Ruth Thomson

Contents

CHILDRENS PRESS®

CHICAGO

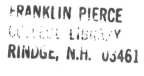

Getting ready

It's fun to make collages.
Collages are pictures made by gluing
different materials and objects
onto a background.

You can make collages with all sorts
of odds and ends.
Start saving scraps of paper
and fabric, aluminum foil, wrapping
paper, string, old magazines,
buttons, and other junk.
Keep them all in a large box.

Collage can be messy.
Cover your table with newspaper.
Wear an old shirt or a smock
to protect your clothes.

3

Paper collage

Get ready

✔ Different kinds of paper   ✔ Glue   ✔ Cardboard

. . . Get Set

Tear some paper into pieces.
Crumple up each piece.
Unfold the pieces
without smoothing out the creases.

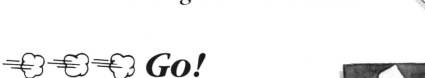

===☁ ===☁ ===☁ *Go!*

Glue the top edge of one piece
of paper to the cardboard.
Pull the rest of the paper into
an interesting shape.
Do the same with the other pieces
of crumpled paper to make a picture.

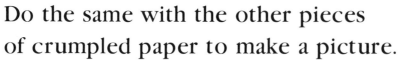

Tissue-paper collage

Get ready

- ✔ Tissue paper in different colors
- ✔ Safety scissors
- ✔ Paste
- ✔ Glue brush
- ✔ Construction paper for mounting

. . . Get Set

Cut or tear tissue paper into shapes.
Torn paper gives a good effect
for trees and animals.
Cut paper is best for buildings
and machines.

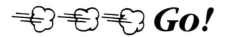 **Go!**

Paste your tissue shapes
onto the construction paper.
You may get some surprises
where different colors overlap.

7

Yarn and string collage

Get ready

✔ Cardboard   ✔ Glue brush   ✔ String

✔ Pencil   ✔ Safety scissors   ✔ Yarn

✔ Glue

. . . Get Set

Draw a design in pencil
on the cardboard.
Keep the outline bold and simple.

≈☁≈☁≈☁ *Go!*

Glue string around the outline.
Decorate the inside of the design
with colored yarn.

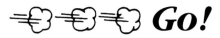

Torn paper mosaic

Get ready

✔ Paper in different colors   ✔ Pencil

✔ Construction paper   ✔ Glue

    for mounting   ✔ Glue brush

. . . Get Set

Draw the outline of a picture
on the construction paper.
Tear the colored papers into pieces.
These are your mosaics.
Keep each color in a separate pile.

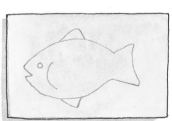

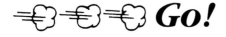

⇶ *Go!*

Arrange the mosaics to fill in your
outline. When you are happy with
them, glue them in place.

11

Stamp mosaic

Get ready

✔ Used stamps
✔ Drawing paper
✔ Pencil or felt-tip pen

✔ Paste
✔ Glue brush

. . . Get Set

Soak used envelopes in water
to loosen the stamps.
Let the stamps dry.
Draw a picture on your paper.

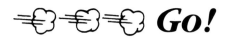 **Go!**

Glue the stamps onto your picture.
Overlap, cut, and tear the stamps
to make an interesting mosaic.

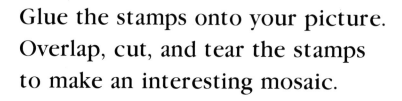

Fabric collage

Get ready

- ✔ Scraps of different kinds of fabric
- ✔ Safety scissors
- ✔ Cardboard
- ✔ White glue
- ✔ Glue brush

. . . Get Set

Cut your scraps of fabric into different shapes.

 *Go!*

Arrange the shapes on the cardboard. Try overlapping them to see what kind of effect you can get. When you are happy with your design, glue the fabric onto the cardboard.

15

Sand collage

Get ready

✔ Cardboard
✔ Pencil
✔ Sand

✔ White glue
✔ Glue brush

. . . Get Set

Draw the outline of a picture or design
on the cardboard in pencil.
Spread glue inside the pencil lines.

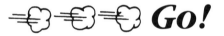 **Go!**

While the glue is still wet,
sprinkle the sand over it.
Make sure all the glue is covered.
Tip any surplus sand off
to see your sand collage.

Button collage

Get ready

✔ Old buttons

✔ Cardboard for mounting

✔ White glue

✔ Glue brush

. . . Get Set

Arrange your buttons on the cardboard to make a picture or a design.

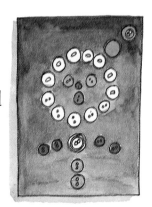

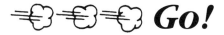 **Go!**

When you are happy with your picture, glue the buttons onto the cardboard. What other interesting designs can you make with buttons?

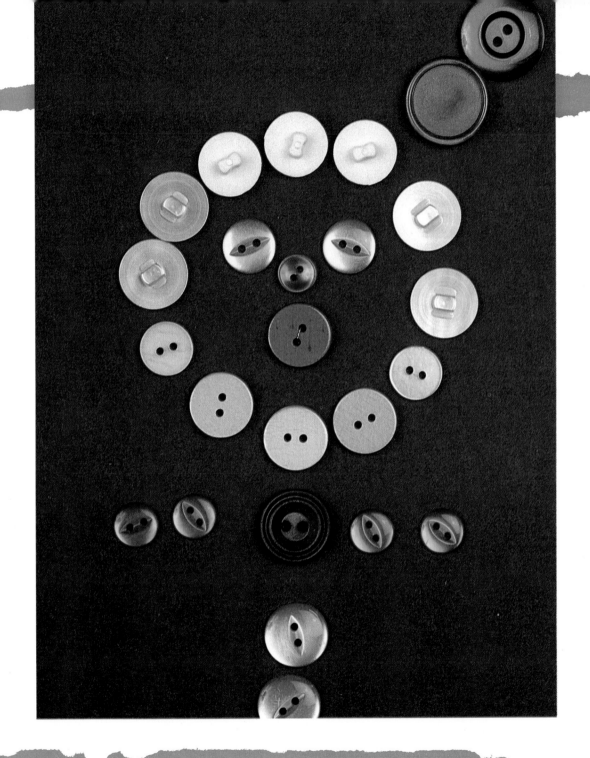

Cork collage

Get ready

✔ Old corks
✔ Knife
✔ Cardboard for mounting

✔ White glue
✔ Glue brush

. . . Get Set

Ask an adult to help you cut
the corks into different lengths.

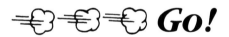 **Go!**

Arrange the cork pieces
on the cardboard.
Glue them down.
What kind of patterns
do the corks make?

Assemblage

Get ready

- ✔ Odds and ends such as net, stickers, stamps, yarn, aluminum foil, feathers, tissue paper
- ✔ Paints and paintbrush
- ✔ Cardboard for mounting
- ✔ White glue
- ✔ Glue brush
- ✔ Safety scissors

. . . Get Set

Paint a simple background on the cardboard.
You may want to draw an outline of your picture as a guide.

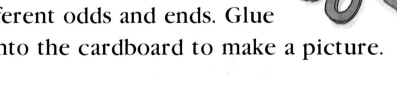

⇒❀⇒❀⇒❀ *Go!*

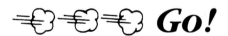

Cut different odds and ends. Glue them onto the cardboard to make a picture.

Index

Library of Congress Cataloging-in-Publication Data

Thomson, Ruth.
    Collage / by Ruth Thomson.
        p.   cm. — (Get set— go!)
    Includes index.
    ISBN 0-516-07988-3
        1. Collage—Juvenile literature. [1. Collage. 2. Handicraft.]
    I. Title. II. Series.
    TT910.T48   1994
    702'.8'12—dc20   94-12305
                                                          CIP
                                                          AC

Photography: Chris Fairclough
Cover photography: John Butcher

Editor: Pippa Pollard
Cover design: Mike Davis
Artwork: Jane Felstead

1994 Childrens Press® Edition
© 1993 Watts Books, London, New York, Sydney
All rights reserved. Printed in the United States of America.
Published simultaneously in Canada.
1 2 3 4 5 6 7 8 9 0 R 03 02 01 00 99 98 97 96 95 94